ABC'S of the SEA

This book belongs to

Dylan Rose

Luke 18:16 "Let the little children come to me
and do not hinder them, for the
kingdom of God belongs to such as these."

For my Perry and Samantha ILU
S.T.C.C.

For Bruce, Jade and Declan Cameron,
my soul inspiration.
C.M.B.

Publisher's Cataloging-in-Publication
(Provided by Quality Books, Inc.)

Celia, Shannon Casey.
   ABC's of the sea / by Shannon Casey Celia ;
illustrations by Carla Bates. — 1st ed.
   p. cm.
   SUMMARY: An alphabet book of words associated with
the sea features linkages to other words starting with
the same letters.
   LCCN 2002090488
   ISBN 0-9718825-0-9 PBC
   ISBN 0-9718825-1-7 HC

   1. Marine animals—Juvenile literature. 2. Boats and
boating—Juvenile literature. 3. English language—
Alphabet—Juvenile Literature. [1. Marine animals.
2. Boats and boating. 3. Alphabet.] I. Title.

QL122.2.C37 2002   591.77
            QBI02-701520

Published by

Mistco, Inc.
P.O. Box 694854
Miami, FL 33269
Phone (305) 653-2003
Fax (305) 653-2037
www.mistco.com

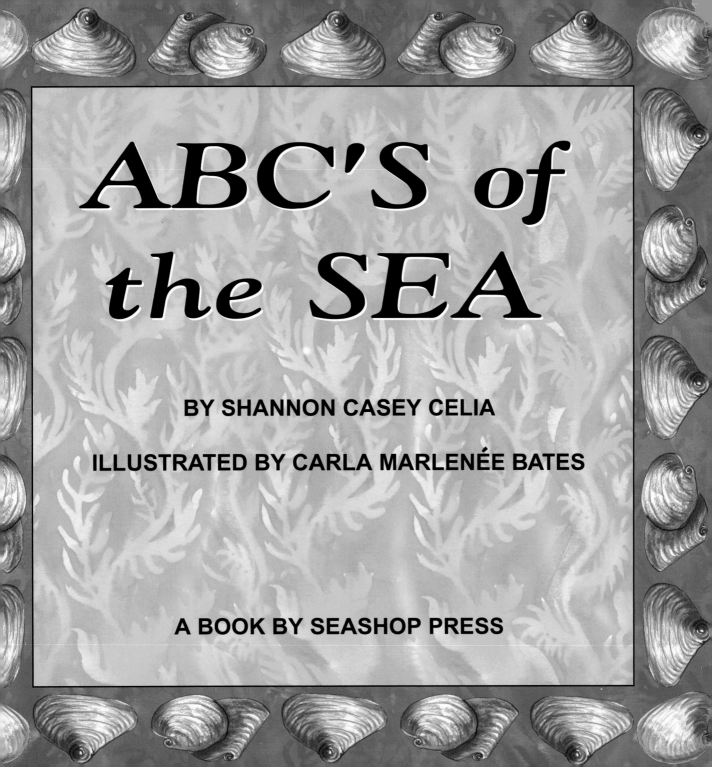

ABC'S of the SEA

BY SHANNON CASEY CELIA

ILLUSTRATED BY CARLA MARLENÉE BATES

A BOOK BY SEASHOP PRESS

Anchor begins with Aa.

Anchors aid ships *adrift*.

Bb is for boat.

Big boats blow by *balmy* beaches.

Crab begins with Cc.

Crawling crabs create *crevices* in sand.

Dd is for **d**olphin.

Diving dolphins *dabble* in the deep.

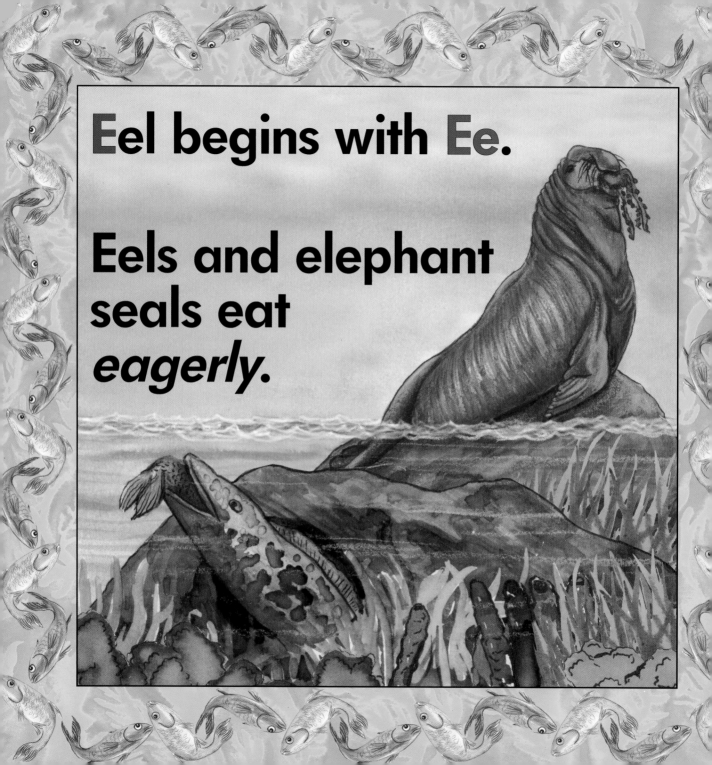

Eel begins with Ee.

Eels and elephant seals eat _eagerly_.

Ff is for fish.

Fantastic fish float with fins.

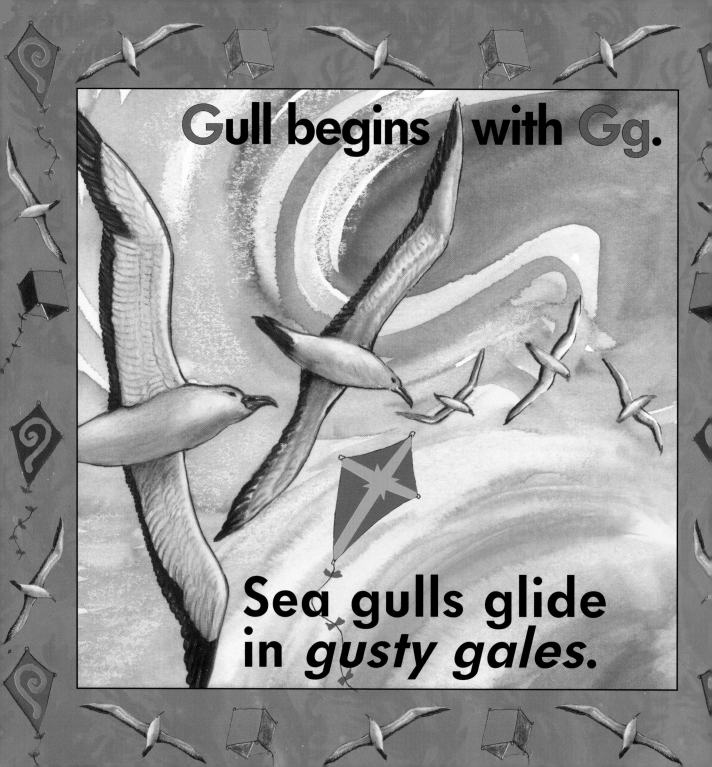

Gull begins with Gg.

Sea gulls glide in *gusty gales*.

Hh is for **h**arbor.

Howling hurricanes are *harsh* on harbors.

Iceberg begins with Ii.

Icebergs *idle* near icy igloos.

Jj is for jellyfish.

Jaunty jellyfish *jiggle* when *jostled.*

Kelp begins with Kk.

Keen kayakers keep away from kelp.

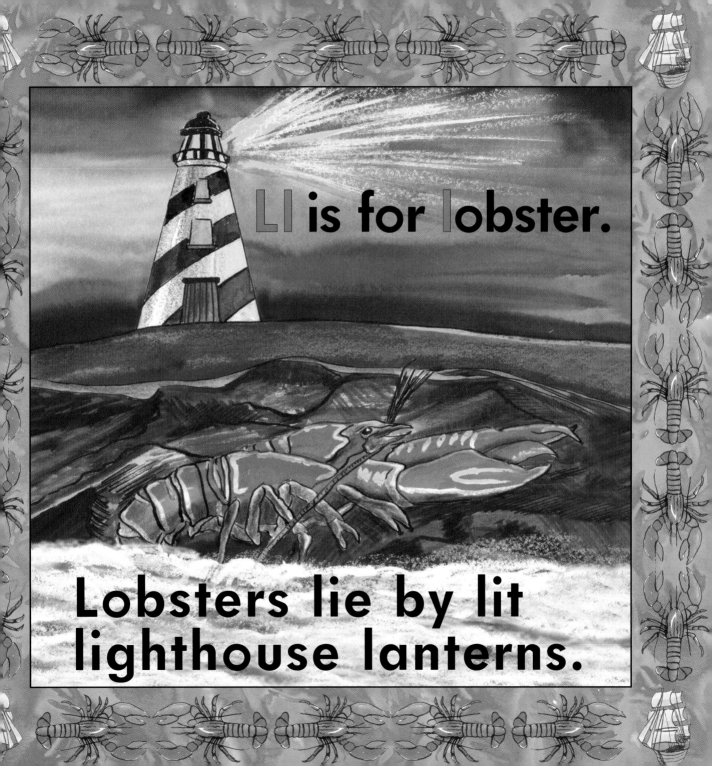

Ll is for lobster.

Lobsters lie by lit lighthouse lanterns.

Mermaid begins with Mm.

Mermaids munch on mackerel by moonlight.

Nn is for nautilus.

Nautiluses navigate near northeastern shores.

Octopus begins with Oo.

Octopuses *oscillate* oddly in oceans.

Pp is for penguin.

Penguins paddle at the South Pole.

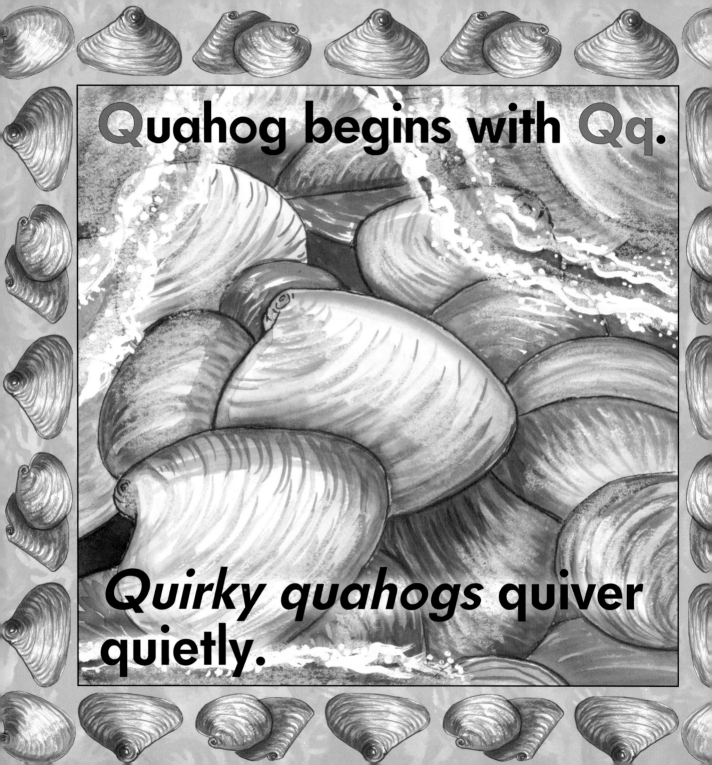

Quahog begins with Qq.

Quirky quahogs quiver quietly.

Rr is for raft.

The raging sea wrecks rickety rafts.

Sea horse begins with Ss.

Sea horses swim near sea stars and sand dollars.

Tt is for turtle.

Tiny turtles toss and turn in the tide.

Urchin begins with Uu.

Unusual sea urchins *cluster* underwater.

Vv is for vessel.

Vast vessels go on voyages.

Whale begins with Ww.

Wide whales wander in the water.

Xx is for xebec.

Sailors on *xebecs* mark their charts with an X.

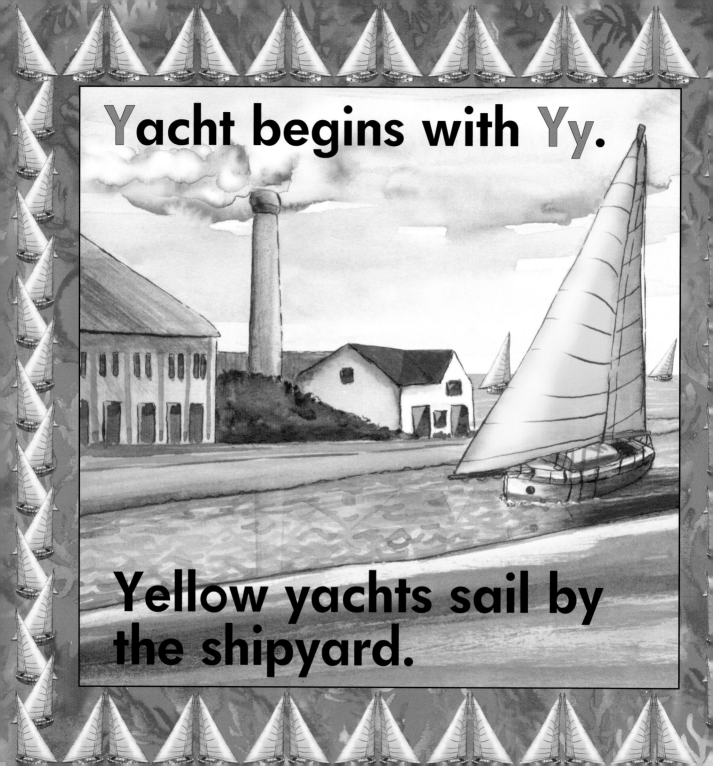

Yacht begins with Yy.

Yellow yachts sail by the shipyard.

Zz is for zebra fish.

Zany zebra fish *zero in* on *zesty* seaweed.

GLOSSARY

Adrift - (a drift') adverb. Freely floating or drifting.

Balmy - (bal' mee) adjective. Comfortable. Pleasantly mild

Cluster - (clus 'ter) verb. To grow or gather in a group or bunch.

Crevice - (crev'is) noun. A small crack or opening.

Dabble - (dab'el) verb. To play in a liquid such as water.

Eagerly - (ee'ger lee) adverb. Really wanting something.

Fantastic - (fan tas' tick) adjective. Incredible. Having an unusual appearance.

Gales - (gails) noun. Powerful winds.

Gusty - (gus' tee) adjective. Sudden bursts of air.

Harsh - (harsh) adjective. Rough or severe.

Idle - (eye' dil) verb. To move without aim.

Jaunty - (jawn' tee) adjective. Perky and carefree.

Jiggle - (jig' el) verb. To make jerky movements.

Jostled - (jos' eld) verb. To be bumped or moved.

Kayaker - (ki' ack ir) noun. A person riding in a narrow boat or canoe called a kayak.

Keen - (keyn) adjective. Smart and wise.

Nautiluses - (naw' ti leses) noun. Sea creatures with multi-chambered spiral shells.

Navigate - (nav' i gait) verb. To move through.

Oscillate - (os' il late) verb. To move back and forth.

Quahogs - (kwa' hogs) noun. East Coast edible clams.

Quirky - (kwir' kee) adjective. Strange, funny or peculiar.

Vast - (vast) adjective. Very large.

Vessels - (ves' ils) noun. Large ships or boats.

Voyage - (voi' ij) noun. A long journey on the ocean.

Xebec - (zee' beck) noun. A small ship with three masts.

Zany - (zay' nee) adjective. Crazy, kooky or silly.

Zero in - (zear' o) (in) verb. To focus on.

Zesty - (zes' tee) adjective. Flavorful.

Aa Bb Cc Dd Ee Ff

Gg Hh Ii Jj Kk Ll Mm

Ss Rr Qq Pp Oo Nn

Tt Uu Vv Ww Xx Yy Zz